EUROPEAN ROOMS IN MINIATURE

INCLUDING A CHINESE AND JAPANESE INTERIOR

by Mrs. James Ward Thorne

THE ART INSTITUTE OF CHICAGO

COVER DESIGN is from *Les Délices des Quatre Saisons,*
French printed cotton of about 1785, by J.-B. Huet

Sixth Edition

Reprinted 1980

Copyright 1948, 1962 by The Art Institute of Chicago

Printed by Hillison & Etten Co., a division of John Blair & Company

Designed by Everett McNear

ISBN 0-86559-002-8

The Miniature Rooms are built to a uniform scale of one inch to the foot, making them one-twelfth actual size. Illustrated is the lacquered pedestal desk and its equipment, used in the early eighteenth-century English library (number 6), shown in comparative scale with a pair of modern spectacles.

FOREWORD

THIS SERIES OF MINIATURE ROOMS, illustrating various phases and types of European interior decorative design since the sixteenth century, was created by Mrs. Thorne after many years of experiment and experience. They were first exhibited in The Art Institute of Chicago in 1937 and attracted wide attention as one of the most popular exhibitions in the Golden Gate International Exposition, San Francisco, in 1939, and the World's Fair of 1940 in New York City.

In order that it might continue to fulfill its educational purpose as widely as possible, this series was presented by Mrs. Thorne to The Art Institute of Chicago in 1941 and was widely circulated through the museums of the country, before it was permanently installed at The Art Institute of Chicago in 1954.

Each room was planned by Mrs. Thorne and carried out under her close personal supervision by a group of expert craftsmen brought together and trained for this special work. Items from Mrs. Thorne's personal collection of miniature objects, some of considerable antiquity and value, have been used whenever they have been found to be of the right type and size. For this she tapped innumerable sources. The occasional book on table or chair, for instance, came from an outstanding English collection. It contains text to

scale! For the most part, however, in order to secure the utmost possible fidelity in scale and design, the furnishings have been made for their particular place, after authentic originals. The rugs were made with few exceptions under Mrs. Thorne's direction by the Needlework and Textile Guild of Chicago.

In certain instances, actual rooms of the period have been reproduced; but in the majority of cases, features from more than one original have been combined or adapted to express more clearly the characteristics of the particular style. It must also be kept in mind that some adjustments have had to be made in order to reproduce a four-walled actuality within the limitations of three visible walls. Some of the devices of the theater have, therefore, been employed to this end.

Few, if any, ancient domestic interiors have survived in their original condition. Individual pieces of furniture have come down to us in quantity, but for their original arrangement we have to rely on the somewhat unreliable evidence of contemporary descriptions and on that of paintings and prints of the period. All these data, however, need interpretation, for which we have no certain clues. According to Hogarth's "Marriage à la Mode" series, for instance, the early Georgian interior was rather clumsily and carelessly arranged. The degree of discrimination displayed in the surviving architecture and furniture must, however, lead us to doubt the artist's interest in the setting beyond his pictorial requirements.

Within certain reasonable limits, therefore, there can be no hard and fast rules for the reconstruction of, say, an eighteenth century living room beyond those dictated by the habits and taste of the period, as far as they are known. Those who would reconstruct such an interior are left largely to the guidance of their own experience and intuition. So-called expert opinions will be found to vary considerably on detail and, therefore, offer little sure help.

Mrs. Thorne has been guided in all this by her own very keen sense of the living quality in any logical arrangement, and also by her obedience to the "theater" which is required in these presentations. They look right; and save in a relatively few matters of detail, it would be difficult, indeed, for the critic to prove his exceptions.

It may be remarked that, in many instances, individual pieces of furniture used are not quite contemporary with the rooms. This gives a true picture of the actuality. A good interior of any age is essentially a living thing which should suggest the time dimension of those who lived in it. A Chippendale chair of 1760 in a room of 1735 does just that, particularly when so recognized.

Thus, in order to fulfill their entire function, these miniature reconstructions have not been limited to strict antiquarian accuracy. Their main purpose, indeed, is the reproduction of an historic style, but dramatic and inspirational appeal is also necessary to enforce the lesson. They should entertain and amuse as well as instruct, and for this some latitude is needful.

It is hardly necessary here to give a verbal tribute to the extraordinary qualities and abilities of the creator of these rooms. The rooms themselves are far more eloquent advocates. Many of the leading art museums of the country would wish, we feel, to join the Art Institute in grateful acknowledgment of Mrs. Thorne's great generosity and zeal in the cause of public education.

The text contained in this volume was prepared by Meyric R. Rogers, and is based on notes and other materials generously placed at the disposal of the writer by Mrs. James Ward Thorne.

1. GREAT HALL

ENGLISH, LATE TUDOR PERIOD, 1550-1600

(HENRY VIII, 1509-1547 — ELIZABETH, 1558-1603)

THE HALL WAS the common living room of the medieval house, serving also as the sleeping quarters of the majority of the male household.

In Tudor times, other living quarters were provided for the "quality," and the hall became mainly the common eating place and the ceremonial gathering place of the household. At this time, the ancient central hearth was moved to the side wall and provided with a chimney. The end of the hall containing the master's table was lighted with a large bay or oriel window, while the entrance way at the other end was sheltered by wood-paneled "screens," through which access was also had to the kitchens and buttery.

Early in the sixteenth century (Henry VIII), the classical motives of the Renaissance began to dilute the traditional medieval or Gothic style. At first, these were drawn directly from Italian sources. Later, these out-side influences came from the Netherlands, which provided the extravagant grotesques and elaborate strapwork (see rail of gallery) characterizing the late Tudor and early Stuart (Jacobean) periods.

This model is mainly a composite of the hall of Wadham College, Oxford, and of that of Parham Park, Sussex. The screens follow those of Wadham and the wall treatment, in general, is taken from Parham Park.

The furniture, with few exceptions, illustrates the types fashionable about 1600—paneled-back benches (settles), "wainscot" chairs, and "melon bulb" turnings on tables and court cupboards. It is arranged in a fashion more representative of a much later date, when the hall had become a reception room for the use of the master and his family and no longer served its original purpose. It is questionable whether many of the accessories—paintings, armor, etc.—while essentially of the appropriate period, would have been so used or placed at the time. The portraits reproduced are of Mary Queen of Scots and the Duchess of Milan, the latter after Holbein.

The floor would usually have been of wood or of flagstones. Marble or stone chequering as shown was more typical of the later seventeenth century.

2. WITHDRAWING ROOM OR BEDROOM

ENGLISH, STUART (JACOBEAN) PERIOD, 1600-1700

(JAMES I, 1603-1625; CHARLES I, 1625-1649; CROMWELL "PROTECTOR," 1649-1660; CHARLES II, 1660-1685; JAMES II, 1685-1688; WILLIAM AND MARY, 1688-1702)

Following, in the main, the so-called Spangle Bedroom of the manor house of Knole, Kent, this room reflects a typical architectural interior of the days of Elizabeth and James I, though the furnishings are practically all of the time of Charles II and even later. This apparent discrepancy does, however, indicate the fact that the Cromwellian wars prevented much building from 1640 to 1660, and most rooms of the Restoration Period (Charles II) were, therefore, actually of this character.

Rooms like this became increasingly numerous in the English house as the importance of the hall declined. The mantelpiece was the decorative focus. Its architectural and carved enrichments, like those of the window embrasures, doorways, etc., contrasted with the relative simplicity of the small rectangular panels of the wainscot.

During this century, oak began to give place to walnut as the favorite furniture wood, though it continued to be used for wall paneling. Here, in fact, everything save the court cupboard against the rear wall and the chest in the right foreground would normally be of walnut, since they are of post-Restoration design (Charles II, James II, and William and Mary), though beech also was extensively used for chairs.

The richly carved woodwork of the Elizabethan bed has given place to an extremely high-canopied, textile-covered bed of a type introduced from France by the court of Charles II. The carpet follows a pattern common in Elizabethan embroidery.

The use of the Flemish scroll in the chairs and also their light construction are chiefly indicative of the radical changes in design which marked the latter part of this century.

Knole House, one of the great surviving Tudor mansions, was presented to the Sackville family by Queen Elizabeth in 1586 and remained in their possession until 1947 when they gave it to the National Trust to be preserved as a public monument.

3. SALON OR RECEPTION ROOM

ENGLISH, STUART PERIOD, 1625-1650

(*CHARLES I, 1625-1649*)

THE MEDIEVAL conservatism of English design was broken largely by the genius of one man. Inigo Jones (1573-1652), a pioneer in the professions of architecture and design, studied in Italy, where he became a disciple of the classicism of Andrea Palladio and an admirer of the richly plastic ornament of the Italian baroque.

On his return to England, he gained the favor of James I, who commissioned him to redesign the royal palace of Whitehall. For the Earl of Pembroke he designed Wilton House in Wiltshire in the new Italian manner. The famous "double cube" room of Wilton established a standard in this style. Jones's work, though stopped by the struggles between King and Parliament, became a potent influence in the English classic movement of the eighteenth century.

It is hard to realize that this model, based very freely on Wilton House, illustrates a style contemporary with that of the model just discussed (No. 2). Damask-covered walls between white and gilded dado and cornice; correct classic orders on doorway, window, and mantel; painted ceiling; and marble floor must have seemed even more cold and garish to people of the times than functional interiors seem to today's conservatives. Such designs were part of a new "thought-out" clarity of plan which was a healthy corrective to the confused picturesqueness of the traditional mode. To such interiors, the heavily carved and gilded furniture of the Italian type was a necessary corollary.

Although sound in theory, such importations were suited neither to the English character nor to the English mode of life and never became so thoroughly naturalized as those brought in later by Sir Christopher Wren.

The "Palladian" window with its triumphal arch motive would have found its normal place opposite the fireplace but necessities of arrangement compelled this readjustment in the model.

The ceiling, elaborately painted in the Italian manner, recalls those in the reception rooms of Wilton. The ornamentation of the deep cove is a simplified version of the original. The center panel merely suggests the type of allegorical painting with which such spaces were usually treated.

4. SALON OR DRAWING-ROOM

ENGLISH, LATE STUART PERIOD, 1670-1700

(CHARLES II, 1660-1685; JAMES II, 1685-1688; WILLIAM AND MARY, 1688-1702)

THE GREAT FIRE OF LONDON in 1666 necessitated the rebuilding of London and gave Sir Christopher Wren his great opportunity. Fortunately, his genius was equal to the challenge. Wren's style, which dominated English decoration and architecture for a century, was based on French and Dutch interpretations of the Classic, and his brick exteriors and wood-paneled interiors appealed immediately to English taste.

This room is adapted from Wren's work in Belton House, Lincolnshire (1685-89). The bold moldings of the oaken paneling and trim make an effective base for the rich naturalistic carving in limewood applied on overmantel and interpanels. These carvings originated with the work of Grinling Gibbons, a Flemish-born artist who set a standard for such work never after excelled. Note also the richly molded plaster work on the ceiling, taken largely from the hall of Belton House.

Both French and Dutch influence is apparent in the furniture. At the end of the century, the richly carved walnut and gilded pieces of the time of Charles II were supplemented by elaborate marquetry in the Dutch fashion of all-over "seaweed" pattern or floral designs, often in many colors.

The S-scroll, either plain or broken, appeared in leg and stretcher. This was the forerunner of the "cabriole" leg, almost universal in the eighteenth century.

Tall case (grandfather) clocks began to be made at this time. The bookcase-top desk and the high chest gradually replaced the earlier standing desk and cabinet.

Under the leadership of Queen Mary, embroidery was much encouraged and came into fashion for draperies, covers, and screens.

The activities of the newly formed East India Company are reflected in the frequent appearance of oriental porcelains as ornaments.

The rug was found in a Paris antique shop, where it had been used as a lamp mat. Soiled beyond recognition, when cleaned it was revealed as a perfect miniature of an oriental weave.

5. COTTAGE INTERIOR

ENGLISH, EIGHTEENTH CENTURY

PARTICULARLY in the south and west of England, thousands of ample farmhouses still exist which testify to the relative prosperity of the English countryside before the Industrial Revolution. This model, a combination of kitchen and living room, is a compilation of many such which may still be found in the Cotswold district and is similar to that in the Anne Hathaway Cottage near Stratford-on-Avon.

The structural beams of the frame construction show as "half timber" in the plastered brick-filled walls. The whole room, excepting the later bay window, is very similar in feeling and structure to those built by the seventeenth-century settler in New England, both being based on the same medieval source.

The furniture, from the seventeenth-century type of settle and stool to the Queen Anne survivals in dresser and chair, is mainly of oak, though elm, walnut, and certain fruitwoods also found a place in these country pieces. The chairs are of the hoop-and-spindle construction widely known as "Windsor," which succeeded the heavy paneling and turning of the wainscot type. Windsors retained their popularity throughout the century. Because of its bending strength, yew was commonly used for the hoops of these chairs. Toward the end of the century, the coarse but often brightly dyed wool stuff used for curtaining was largely replaced by cotton prints or chintzes.

Though cooking and other household work was carried on in these kitchens, much of the heavier and dirtier work was consigned to the scullery, leaving the kitchen essentially a living room. The dresser became a means of display as well as utility. Shelves of pewter and earthenware replaced the earlier wooden ware which had been retired also to the scullery. The appearance of Toby jugs and other figured wares marked the beginning of the later so-called "cottage ornaments." The floor of flagging indicates that it was laid directly on the ground, cellars or basements being practically unknown. The chill of these floors, which in the earlier days was relieved by strewing them with rushes or sweet herbs, was now combated with homemade rugs of hooked or braided form.

6. LIBRARY

ENGLISH, FIRST HALF OF THE EIGHTEENTH CENTURY

Like the previous room, it is difficult to give this interior a more precise dating. The paneling itself is of a type used in less important rooms during the first half of the eighteenth century. The secondary character of the room is indicated by its lack of symmetry. Such a wide window opening, in all likelihood, would have been occasioned only by the need of accommodating an ancient broad casement window. This has apparently been replaced by a later sash type. Boldly fielded paneling such as this was seldom made after the time of George I.

With the exception of the corner cupboard which is later in type, the furniture is all of the style prevalent during the first quarter of the century. Typical are the hoop-back chairs with their broad, boldly scrolled back splats and cabriole legs ending in claw-and-ball or pad feet. Walnut was in almost universal use except in the case of the lacquered pieces, which were usually of pine or other soft wood. When particularly fine grain was desired, the walnut was laid on in veneers over a hardwood base.

During this period tea drinking and card playing both became popular social amenities. This is reflected by the appearance of small tables adapted to these functions. Note the tray top table near the fireplace designed to hold the tea service and on the extreme right a folding card table, the corners of the top rounded to receive candlesticks. Beside the leather covered wing chair is one type of candle stand and another, both with tripod bases, by the side chair in the foreground. Candlesticks thus supported and wall brackets or sconces furnished the usual artificial lighting of secondary rooms.

The green used here in the paneling was a favorite during this period. White paneling came into vogue only during the last years of the century.

The curious may be interested to know that the portrait on the left wall is a miniature of Lucy, Countess of Sussex, painted in oil on wood, and the effective landscape hung over the fireplace was originally the cover of an old card case.

7. DRAWING-ROOM

ENGLISH, EARLY GEORGIAN PERIOD, ABOUT 1735

(GEORGE II, 1727-1760)

No SINGLE SOURCE can be given for this room though some of its features, the niches and the doorway, are taken, with changes in scale, from those in the Hatton Garden Room in the Victoria and Albert Museum, London.

By and large, it represents those developments in the Wren tradition instituted by his pupil, James Gibbs, and popularized later in the publications of Batty Langley and Abraham Swan. The scale of carving and moldings is finer and more conventional. There is a striving for greater elegance in proportion but there is also a loss in character compared with the earlier type.

Such rooms were commonly made of pine and painted in green, blue or a reddish tan, sometimes with the ornament picked out in gold, though when of clear "deal" as in this instance, it is possible they were sometimes left in the natural wood. Deal is the common English term for pine or fir.

This was a period of great building activity when actually thousands of the ancient country houses of England were either completely rebuilt or radically altered to conform to the new Palladian manner promoted by an aristocratic architectural cult led by Lord Burlington and his protegé, William Kent. The Kent manner is reflected in some features of this room, the ceiling in particular, and in the eagle console tables derived from Italian sources.

The furniture in mahogany, with the above exceptions, shows forms typical of the early Chippendale or pre-Chippendale eras. The needlework rug follows an occidental type.

Those curious as to the "know-how" of miniature reproduction will be interested to learn that the "porcelains" in the niches are of ivory. The jades on the mantel shelf are actually Chinese, as is also the "Coromandel" screen.

The decorative use to which the fine portraits of the mid-eighteenth century were put is shown by the "Gainsborough" framed in the overmantel.

8. BEDROOM

ENGLISH, GEORGIAN PERIOD, "CHINESE-CHIPPENDALE," 1760-1775

(GEORGE III, 1760-1820)

THE COMBINATION of the rococo forms adopted from France and Italy by Thomas Chippendale and his contemporaries with the European craze for orientalisms, which reached its height in the mid-eighteenth century, produced what is known in England as the Chinese-Chippendale style. With it came the straight square leg and the pierced fret, both derived from Chinese furniture.

Chinese painted wall paper and its European block-printed substitutes were, in general, taking the place of wood paneling. Color schemes were being lightened and full advantage was taken of the informalities possible with the style. The freedom and fantasy which it offered were the causes both of the style's popularity and its rapid decay, and also its constant revival whenever free decoration came again into fashion.

This particular room follows with slight changes one from Wotton-under-Edge, Gloucestershire, dating from about 1760, now in the Victoria and Albert Museum, London. The gilded mirror and mirrored sconces or girandoles were made after a design given in Chippendale's "Gentleman and Cabinet Maker's Director" first issued in 1754. The bed follows a published example from Tabley House, Cheshire, dated about 1760. As in the case of the other furnishings of the room, it is exquisitely made, both in scale and finish.

The gay and amusing treatment of the overmantel shows a favorite eighteenth century method of using the little white or polychrome Chinese figurines so much in demand. It demonstrates how well the informality of these little figures harmonizes with the rococo scroll work.

The Chinese fret has even been carried into the fireplace fittings.

The tall stands or torcheres in the windows were customarily used to support candelabra.

9. SALON OR DRAWING-ROOM

ENGLISH, GEORGIAN PERIOD, ''HEPPLEWHITE,'' 1770-1780

(GEORGE III, 1760-1820)

THE SEVERE CLASSICISM of this composite room reflects that Palladianism of the Lord Burlington type which held its ground stanchly against the rococo inroads of the mid-eighteenth century. Except for the furniture, such a room might have been built almost any time between 1735 and 1765.

The mantel and overmantel are, however, more definitely of the first half of the century.

For the most part, the furniture is of a style generally assigned to George Hepplewhite and his contemporaries, which was a skillful Anglicization of the French types of 1760-1775, transitional between those of Louis XV and Louis XVI. The commodes, the small tables, and the oval-back armchairs are representative. The other pieces belong to the rectilinear designs of the later Sheraton or Hepplewhite-Sheraton phase, though the "shield-back" side chairs are always considered a peculiarly Hepplewhite construction or development. Since such forms as the drum-top table, the "sofa" table, and even the secretary are of the decade of 1790-1800, we might extend the dates of the whole to the latter year.

In the lacquered commodes flanking the fireplace and in the armchairs and tabouret on the right, we see the strong influence of the French Louis XV style on English taste of this period (1760-1780) which is evident in Hepplewhite's designs.

The rug is a reproduction of an English piece of the Aubusson type.

It should be remembered that Hepplewhite's book, published in 1789, three years after his death, and also Chippendale's, published in 1754, were trade catalogues of contemporary fashions rather than the sole inventions of their authors. Thomas Sheraton's publication of 1792 was probably somewhat more in advance of the current styles since he was a draughtsman rather than a cabinetmaker.

10. DINING ROOM

ENGLISH, GEORGIAN PERIOD, "ADAM," 1770-1790

(GEORGE III, 1760-1820)

ABOUT THE MIDDLE of the eighteenth century, excavations in the Græco-Roman resort cities of Herculaneum and Pompeii, buried at the beginning of the Christian era, caused not only great excitement in artistic circles but considerable changes in the current concept of what classic decoration really was.

The young Scottish architect, Robert Adam, thoroughly saturated with these new ideas during his studies in Italy and Dalmatia, returned to London about 1760 to practice architecture with his brother James. The precision, effectiveness, and novelty of his designs gained him immediate recognition. For a quarter of a century, Robert Adam became, in fact, the dictator of arts and taste in England.

Like Inigo Jones in the seventeenth century, the Brothers Adam, to insure perfect conformity, undertook to design not only the house and its interior, but everything that went into it. The furniture designs with which he supplied cabinetmakers like Chippendale were based largely on the blending of contemporary Italian fashions with current English forms. In interior treatment, he discarded wood and paper for paint and plaster, working out most of the ornament in low relief in the manner of the ancient Græco-Roman stuccos, against a toned plaster ground in framed or unframed panels.

The method is well shown in this room which uses motives from various rooms in Home House, London (1774-78), and in Saltram, Devonshire, both by Robert Adam.

The fine-scale precision of this style is in sharp contrast with the previous fashions. Its over-refinement tended, however, to a dryness which finally brought the style into disfavor.

Much of the furniture designed by Adam was gilded in the Continental fashion. Mahogany was often parcel-gilded; that is, the ornament was picked out in gold, as in the case of this side table and its accompanying pedestals and urns—the immediate ancestor of the sideboard. The pedestal extension dining table is a typical development of the period. Furniture veneered with light colored woods such as satinwood, sycamore, etc. was frequently used and usually decorated with marquetry or painting.

11. ENTRANCE HALL AND STAIRWAY

ENGLISH, GEORGIAN PERIOD, ABOUT 1775

(GEORGE III, 1760-1820)

THIS UNIT is based mainly on the entrance hall of No. 1, Bedford Square, London, designed by Thomas Leverton. The foreground section has here been changed to follow a design of Leverton's contemporary, James Wyatt. In the original, the saucer dome from which the lantern hangs is itself supported on pendentives or sections of another dome.

This composite interior does, in fact, represent two phases of the Adam style as interpreted by his contemporaries. One part shows a personal simplification of the Roman stucco forms influenced by the Louis XVI style. The other shows a reliance upon painted arabesque decoration long popular in Italy since the time of Raphael but here sharpened and lightened by a restudy of classic originals found in Pompeii and Herculaneum. The importation of such decorators as Cipriani and Angelica Kauffmann widely popularized this type of treatment.

The furniture shown is in what may be called the Adam-Hepplewhite style.

The cameo plaques forming candle sconces are actually miniature pieces of Wedgwood jasperware.

Note the circular rug which "echoes" the design of the dome above.

The extremely delicate execution of this model needs no comment.

12. DRAWING-ROOM

ENGLISH, GEORGIAN PERIOD, "SHERATON," ABOUT 1800

(GEORGE III, 1760-1820)

THIS SIMPLE ROOM illustrates the effect of Robert Adam and his imitators on less pretentious interiors. Their influence is visible in the mantelpiece and the slender pilasters above, and in the trim of doorway and window. The wall treatment could be of wood or might be carried out in plaster, the latter being more in keeping with the times.

With the exception of the two side chairs, all the furniture is of the type that has been given the name of Thomas Sheraton (1750-1806), though he was probably more influential in retrospect than in actuality (see No. 9).

In general, "Sheraton" furniture, before the style came under French "Empire" influence, is distinguished by its lightness in both weight and color. Satinwood, sycamore, and other light-colored woods supplemented or replaced mahogany at this time. Satinwood veneers lent themselves to marquetry and to painting. Carving practically disappeared and furniture tended toward extreme delicacy, becoming at the same time somewhat dry in form and line, and its decoration mechanical.

The rug follows a typical Aubusson of English design.

13. ROTUNDA AND LIBRARY

ENGLISH, GEORGIAN PERIOD, "REGENCY," 1810-1820

(GEORGE IV, REGENT FOR GEORGE III, 1811-1820)

THE FIRST DECADES of the nineteenth century reflected even in England the fact that Napoleon was attempting the revival of Imperial Rome in furniture and decoration as well as in all other fields.

Under the architect, Sir John Soane, the English version of this movement infused a new monumentality into the Adam classic, yet this period also saw a new freedom in ornament and design which reached its height in the extravagances of the Brighton Pavilion built for George IV.

This room illustrates the conservative side of the style which, in its humbler aspects, was paralleled by the "Biedermeier" fashions in central Europe and by the so-called "Phyfe" style in America.

The model is a combination of two interiors. The rotunda, presumably based on a design by Soane, is somewhat lighter than his usual style. The principal feature of the library beyond is taken from a bookcase in Kenwood, a famous house outside London, designed by Robert Adam in 1767.

The inspiration for most of the furniture of this period was evidently directly drawn from bronzes and marbles of Roman times. When no definite precedent existed, a suitably "imperial" form was contrived to suit. In addition to mahogany with a reddish finish, considerable ebony or black lacquer was used with gilded or brass mounts and inlays.

Accents of strong color were usual in draperies and covers, and there was liberal use of gold and gilding.

Rugs of the period were designed to recall the arrangement of Roman floor mosaics but in heavy color quite different from the muted tones of the late eighteenth century.

14. DRAWING-ROOM

ENGLISH, VICTORIAN PERIOD, 1840-1870

(QUEEN VICTORIA, 1837-1901)

THE VICTORIAN PERIOD covers a multitude of successive fashions and "revivals" which are difficult to place in strict chronological order. The traditional disciplines of the crafts in matters of design were rapidly swept away before a combination of ill-considered romanticism and the mechanical resources of the age. Patronage had largely escaped from the aristocracy into the hands of the new industrialist class who were intrigued by the curious and the intricate.

In spite of the "confusion of tongues" in things artistic, much was structurally sound. Many Victorian ensembles have a sort of opulent picturesqueness and a nostalgic warmth though they violate what is generally accepted as good design.

This model, based on no single original, is less cluttered than might be expected. Tomato red carpet and draperies against green walls give the usual color range with the black lacquer and gilding and the rosewood, walnut, or dark mahogany of the furniture.

Architecturally, such rooms are nondescript: a ceiling recalling the Renaissance, a baroque and rococo parentage for mantel and windows, and a diluted echo of the "Chippendale Gothic" on the walls show a complete disregard of stylistic propriety.

Reproductions of portraits of Queen Victoria and Prince Albert by Hayter and Winterhalter and Baxter Prints of Osborne and Balmoral are but restrained tokens of the plethora of pictures which garnished the average nineteenth-century house.

In studying such interiors, it is difficult to distinguish between feelings of affection and of irritation.

15. DRAWING-ROOM

ENGLISH, CONTEMPORARY

THIS ROOM rounds the cycle of three centuries of English decorative style between Henry VIII and the uncrowned Edward VIII.

Comparing the model with those preceding it, we see that, in its essentials, it recalls and adapts to contemporary ideas the eighteenth-century traditions of Wren, Adam, and Soane. Its virtues are in its simplifications but in spite of the resources and flexibility of modern lighting, it also typifies the weakness of much modified traditional design in its lack of logical or imaginative handling of detail.

The essential traditionalism of the British approach, which is not without well-seated wisdom, is seen in the furniture. This, with the exception of the blocky, overstuffed, club pieces and the hint of functionalism in glass and chromium, is pure eighteenth-century Chippendale or a close adaptation of it.

The blue and silver color scheme in sharply divided masses is typical of the chic but somewhat theatrical use of color prevalent today.

The room, which is keyed, so to speak, by the portrait of the Duke of Windsor, shown in his royal robes during his brief career as Edward VIII, contains some remarkable examples of miniature reproduction. Note the smoking equipment and the copy of "Country Life," which can be read with the aid of a magnifying glass.

Through the doorway to the right, a glimpse may be had of a dining room in gold and black with a table set with all the most up-to-date equipment of the late 1930's. Through the open French windows may be seen the twinkling lights across Regents Park.

It is not by pure chance that the room is shown by artificial light at night. First gas and then electricity have made it possible for us to use the house after nightfall to a degree unknown in earlier centuries. Social life has largely shifted from day to night and, in consequence, artificial illumination has begun to play an ever more important part in our design for living.

16. HALL OR "SALLE"

FRENCH, PERIOD OF LOUIS XII, ABOUT 1500

(LOUIS XII, 1498-1515)

THE GREAT semi-fortified chateaux of the Loire Valley represent, in general, the transition between the feudal Gothic times and the new ideas of the Renaissance then filtering northward from Italy. Externally, for the most part, they were still the grim strongholds of an earlier day but in the interior, large windows and a growing propensity for display furniture already showed the change to a more ample life that was taking place and a decreasing need for constant vigilance against armed attack.

This movement is expressed in this model, which is based on but does not reproduce similar interiors in such chateaux as Chaumont and Langeais. The Renaissance tendency to emphasize the fireplace is evident even if its detail is still Gothic. Paneling of late Gothic design warms the lower part of the walls and is interrupted or developed on one side into a canopied seat of honor and on the other into an elaborate sideboard or *dressoir* for the display of plate.

With the exception of the two paneled-back chairs flanking the fireplace, the rest of the wood furniture is already in the new Italian mode. The metalwork, particularly the candle stand and lectern in the foreground, is, however, completely medieval in form.

The tapestry reproductions made in Vienna in fine point embroidery are somewhat later in style but represent the early verdure types which were used to supplement wood paneling in relieving the harshness of the stone walls.

On the manteling of the fireplace, which closely follows that of Chaumont, are reproduced the porcupine and ermine—the emblems of Louis XII and his Queen, Anne of Brittany. Their initials are also shown above.

Though the miniature replicas on the *dressoir* are mostly of a later date, they represent the gold and silver plate which was displayed in accord with the rank and importance of the owner. According to the sumptuary laws of the time the higher the rank of the owner the more shelves he was permitted to use.

17. BEDROOM

FRENCH, PERIOD OF THE VALOIS, LATE SIXTEENTH CENTURY

(FRANCIS I, 1515-1547; HENRY II, 1547-1559; CHARLES IX, 1560-1574; HENRY III, 1574-1589)

DURING THE REIGN of Francis I, the influx of Italian forms and ornament definitely brought the Renaissance to France. The painted and gilded leather wall covering and the painted and beamed ceiling reproduced mainly from the chateau of Azay-le-Rideau and the fireplace adapted from one in the Chateau of Loches all represent this period. The device of Francis I—the salamander—appears on the overmantel.

The room as a whole, however, must be taken to represent such an interior as it may have been at the end of the century or even later. The furniture, with the exception of the two Gothic "joint" stools and the paneled-back chair near the bed, is all of the second half of the century or the early part of the seventeenth. The leather-backed "Spanish" chair, the spiral-turned armchair, and the high-back chair with scroll arms must all be given definitely to the period of Louis XIII.

The two cabinets, called *armoires à-deux-corps*, are copied from examples in the Cluny Museum in Paris. The right-hand one is particularly famous as it is said to have come from the abbey of Cluny itself.

With the exception of the Gothic pieces, the furniture is all of walnut.

The portrait on the left wall is actually a miniature painting, but of a later style and date.

The draped bed is also of a seventeenth-century type.

The continued use of tapestry as a wall covering is seen through the doorway in the rear.

18. SALON

(LOUIS XIV, 1643-1715)

DURING THE LONG REIGN of the "Sun King," the decorative and architectural forms of the high Renaissance and baroque styles of Italy were absorbed and transformed into a truly national French style which, in its time, dominated the rest of Europe.

This rather overwhelmingly florid yet ornamental style, to which we now give the name of the monarch, was devised by many artists of genius working under the direction of Charles LeBrun (1619-1690) to give a setting proper to a despot whose subservient court was made up of all the proudest feudal nobility of France. The classic orders were employed with great effect. Paneled ceilings framed in deep coves gave additional height and splendor. Practically all relief ornament, whether in wood or plaster, was heavily gilded. Much use was made of mirrors to increase the effect of illumination.

This room might well represent a small antechamber in one of the great reception suites which made up most of the great palace of Versailles or in another of the many splendid royal chateaux built or rebuilt during the second half of the century.

The massive gilded furniture, scrolled and carved, still shows its Italian inspiration. The two heavy cabinets or commodes against the window wall are in the style of André Charles Boulle, who developed a veneer technique in tortoise shell, ebony, and gilded bronze which still bears his name.

Above the fireplace is a full-length portrait of Louis XIV in his robes of state reproduced in miniature from the original by Hyacinthe Rigaud.

The rug suggests the famous pile *Savonnerie* of the period.

The royal emblems of the intertwined "L's" and the head with sun rays are used as decorative motives here as in all royal buildings of the time.

The two K'ang-hsi porcelains on the Boulle commodes are reminders of the craze for collecting oriental porcelains which was started in France by the famous minister of Louis XIII, Cardinal Richelieu, and Cardinal Mazarin, his successor.

Against the marble walls of the hallway in the rear hangs a pictorial tapestry typical of the period.

19. DINING ROOM

FRENCH, PERIOD OF LOUIS XIV, 1660-1700

(LOUIS XIV, 1643-1715)

THE PALATIAL STYLE of Louis XIV had a less gorgeous and more liveable side which is illustrated in this oak-paneled interior suggested by the designs of Jules-Hardouin Mansart for the Grand Trianon, Versailles. Similar designs were made throughout the second half of the century but its simplicity and relative severity indicate, in this instance, a date about 1680, when the last traces of the Louis XIII style vanished before the first signs of the approaching *rococo* of the eighteenth century.

It was this style that had a great influence on the later work of Wren in England (see No.4, Belton House), both directly, and through Holland, by the agency of Daniel Marot (1650-1712), a French designer appointed architect to William III.

The rather somber color of the room is relieved by gilding and the multi-toned inlays of the furniture, the red and gold of the velvet brocade upholstery, and the velvet hangings.

The miniature rug was embroidered in wool in order to simulate the pile texture of the *Savonnerie* of the time. Note that the design of the ceiling is partially "reflected" in that of the rug.

The table and buffet or sideboard follow designs of Jean Le Pautre (1618-1682). Jean, his brother Antoine, and his son Pierre (d. 1716) constituted a family of engravers and designers who played an important part in the formation of the Louis XIV style in both its early and late phases.

The rest of the furniture is also in the formal style of the period, about 1675.

20. LIBRARY

(LOUIS XV, 1715-1774; PERIOD OF THE REGENCY, 1715-1723)

THE BRIEF REGENCY of Philippe d'Orléans gives its name to this style of transition between the baroque classic of Louis XIV and the true rococo of the second quarter of the eighteenth century.

This transitional style retains the forms and architectural outlines of the earlier period but introduces the free S- and C-scrolls into the included ornament in a strictly symmetrical arrangement. Elliptical curves also appear at door and panel heads.

In its more restrained phase as illustrated here, this style has a balanced grace and dignity which make it preëminent among the French styles of the Bourbon period. The paneling, usually of oak, was generally painted with the ornament parcel-gilded. Occasionally, it was left unpainted and the ornament gilded only. Much period paneling is now seen stripped of the successive coats of paint which, in the course of time, obscured the delicacy of its carvings.

The overdoor and over-panel paintings are typical of the eighteenth century style.

The furniture is also all of types in vogue during the first years of Louis XV. Its lines are flowing yet ample and dignified in effect. The writing table follows one of the most beautiful designs of the century. The wood of the chairs was usually painted or gilded, while the tables and "case" pieces were veneered in exotic woods and accented with mounts of gilded bronze (ormolu).

The miniature paintings and portraits are in the style of François Boucher, 1703-1770.

Some of the small accessories are miracles of workmanship and all are beautifully in scale—an extraordinary accomplishment.

The rug follows a design of the period.

21. BOUDOIR

FRENCH, PERIOD OF LOUIS XV, 1740-1760

(*LOUIS XV, 1715-1774*)

As the Regency style passed into the full rococo of the mid-century, the earlier architectural forms lost importance, save for the panel moldings. Panels blossomed at head and base into freely drawn clusters of scroll, shell and strange floral forms exquisitely carved. Actual symmetry was often discarded in favor of a freedom that echoed the general relaxation of the social restraints of the past.

It was, as far as the prosperous were concerned, an age of comfort. Chairs were constructed for reclining rather than sitting, and couches and sofas multiplied. Small tables and cabinets became numerous and ingenious dressing tables were designed to accommodate the needs of the elaborate toilets of the time.

Oriental porcelains were now supplemented by products of European potters, who had rediscovered the secrets of kaolin.

While the materials used in the furniture changed little, preference was given to lighter tones, both in woods and draperies as well as in paints. Gilding was more silvery and muted colors such as rose, lilac, cool apple greens, and powder blue began to predominate. White was, however, seldom used until toward the end of the century when it became almost universal as a wall color.

The taste of the day was very considerably formed by the preferences of Mme. de Pompadour, who exercised far more power than the Queen, Marie Leszczynska, whose portrait, with that of Louis XV, hangs on the rear wall.

Mme. de Pompadour ruled Louis XV and France more by her skill and personality than by her beauty and was definitely a constructive influence in matters concerning the arts.

Many of the miniature accessories appearing in this French room were found in Paris antique shops which specialize in this Lilliputian material.

The marble mantel is somewhat higher in relation to the paneling than usual in this period.

22. BEDROOM AND BOUDOIR

FRENCH (NORMANDY), EIGHTEENTH CENTURY

(*LOUIS XVI, 1774-1793*)

In a sense, this re-creation of a Normandy manor house interior parallels that of the English cottage interior (No. 5). In this case, however, it reflects the life of a class a little higher in the social scale.

Homes of this type were citadels of conservatism. Such a room, though the major part of the furnishings is Louis XV in type, belongs actually to the following period. Some of the chairs which show definite indications of the Louis XVI era—the lyre-back, for instance, are, in fact, only a decade or so later than the fine provincial armoire or wardrobe on the window wall with its profusely carved door panels in the full Louis XV manner.

In such interiors—just as in the simpler homes of the time in America—wall paneling was often confined to one wall, as here, where it enclosed the bed alcove, which is just one stage removed from the built-in box bed of universal peasant tradition. The beamed ceiling suggests that this represents the refurbishing of an earlier structure.

The remaining walls are covered with a skillful reproduction of a charming sprigged wall paper, recalling the designs of Pillement, such as the early French wall paper makers produced as an inexpensive substitute for the elegant hand painted paper of the Orient.

The furniture used would probably be of oak. It long retained its popularity in Normandy and Brittany after walnut was in general use elsewhere.

The rugs, reproducing the *gros point* homemade type of the period, were originally a handbag and the top of a powder box found in Paris shops.

23. DINING ROOM

FRENCH, PERIODS OF LOUIS XV AND XVI, 1760-1780

(LOUIS XV, 1715-1774; LOUIS XVI, 1774-1793)

THE DOUBLE DATE in the title is an indication that the abandonment of the rococo in favor of a new classicism was already in process almost fifteen years before the accession of Louis XVI, whose name has been attached to this style. In many ways, the movement was a return to the traditional French classicism of Louis XIV but with an almost feminine refinement and delicacy in scale and ornament (see Nos. 19 and 20).

This interior, modeled after a room in one of the smaller houses in Fontainebleau, seems to belong to the earlier phase of the style as shown in the engraved designs of the younger Boucher and Lalonde. Later the style tended to become either too fussy and delicate or too coldly academic. Here, there is a sense of restfulness and ease.

Colors during these years became even more muted toward tones of gray. An off-white relieved with gilded ornaments and moldings was a favorite scheme closely seconded by the greenish gray seen here.

The character of the architecture was echoed in the furniture which became much simpler in form and line, though still richly carved.

The preference for delicate textures was carried out in the rugs, which were predominantly of tapestry weave as produced in the factory at Aubusson.

The form and design of the dining table is somewhat questionable since a small round table was the typical dining equipment of the eighteenth century. Multiple units were used if necessary. The use of a long extension table in the "English fashion" was an innovation of the period but long fixed tables as shown here were practically unknown.

The "Houdon" busts on the console tables were deftly converted from miniature reproductions originally made as silver seals.

24. BOUDOIR OR "SALON"

FRENCH, PERIOD OF LOUIS XVI, ABOUT 1780

(LOUIS XVI, 1774-1793)

IN DELICACY, the acme of the Louis XVI style is generally considered to have been reached in the series of private rooms built into the palaces of Versailles, the Petit Trianon, and Fontainebleau, during the last years of the reign of Louis XV.

While many of these are even smaller in scale than this little salon, it represents the less formal setting in which the young Marie Antoinette loved to escape from the restraints of court etiquette. In comparison with contemporary state apartments, it shows the same striving for a simpler and more intimate life that found its ultimate expression in the "Hamlet"—a romantic village—built on the grounds of the Trianon, where the Queen and her friends played at farm life.

Here formal architectural features have been fined down to the point of being hardly more than decorative motives. "Trophies" of garden tools, musical instruments, etc., carved on the panel heads, are indicative of the same spirit.

The marble-topped commode and fall-front secretary are beautifully made antique models, which were fortunate finds in Paris. The pictures, which are all miniatures on ivory, are indicative of the fashion for small paintings and knick-knacks which later developed into the clutter of the Victorian age. The "tapestry" of the upholstery and rug is rendered in the finest needlepoint.

As in the Louis XV period, a large proportion of the chairs were painted rather than gilded.

25. BATHROOM AND BOUDOIR

FRENCH, PERIOD OF THE REVOLUTION, 1793-1804

(THE DIRECTORATE AND THE CONSULATE)

For want of a better term, we have used the "Period of the Revolution" to signify the interval between the fall of the monarchy and the coronation of Napoleon. In spite of the turbulence of these times, a series of brief decorative fashions developed which presaged the Empire style while retaining much of the delicacy of their predecessor. These fashions all attempted to symbolize the republicanism of the day by resorting to what were commonly accepted as the decorative forms of Roman republicanism. The wall decorations of Pompeii and Herculaneum were adopted for this purpose following the intense interest aroused by the excavation of these buried cities after 1748.

The model is adapted, both in form and color, from designs in the Pompeian manner made for a certain Mlle. Dervieux by the architect Belanger, who had also designed Bagatelle for the brother of the late King, but had escaped the Jacobin fury after a brief period in prison.

Unfortunately, the taste and tact as well as "chic" with which such designs were conceived did not long survive the growing urge for display which led to absurd extravagance in both decoration and costume.

Classic motives taken from ancient vases and frescoes, and bird and animal forms of mythological significance entirely replaced the floral, pastoral, and cultural motives dear to the old regime. Painted ornament served the rapidly changing modes more readily and effectively than could any modeled forms.

Color, in obedience to the remains of frescoes and mosaics, again became strong and positive—earth reds and yellows and black again appeared.

Furniture followed a similar path and often succeeded in attaining most effective combinations of presumably correct archaeology with a delicacy of line inherited from the earlier period. Ebony and light fruitwoods shared popularity with mahogany and gilded finishes.

26. ANTEROOM OR SALON

FRENCH, PERIOD OF THE EMPIRE, ABOUT 1810

(NAPOLEON BONAPARTE, EMPEROR, 1804-1814)

IN ITS BROADER DESIGN, this room differs but slightly from the more severe type of Louis XVI interior. The detail, particularly in the ornament, belongs, however, definitely to the unsympathetic and rigid but nonetheless imposing type of the Empire. In its materials also—the overall use of marbles or marbleized plaster in markedly contrasting tones—it demonstrates the effort toward formality and obvious richness characteristic of the style. Paneling, which always suggests wood, is conspicuously absent save in the doors. All the wall surfaces are treated with the idea of simulating the Imperial Roman method of marble veneer on a core of brick masonry. With few exceptions, the ornament is made to give at least the appearance of gilded bronze applied to the marble surface.

It should also be noted that Egyptian motives such as the Sphinx are mingled with those of Rome. Such motives became more common after the Napoleonic campaigns in Egypt.

More strident colors came into general use. Gold on black or mahogany red in the furniture, gold on crimson damask for upholstery and drapes, and again gold on a base of rich brown in the rugs constituted a typical color scheme in which deep blue or green easily took the place of red.

Amid the splendors of imperial symbolism, grace of line and form was generally forgotten. In the designs of Percier and Fontaine, the leading exponents of the style and the official architects to Napoleon, there was, however, a great degree of refinement and a decorative inventiveness seldom found in the work of their imitators.

Students of architecture and decoration will find it profitable to study comparatively the work of Percier and Fontaine, and that of the Brothers Adam in England.

27. LIBRARY OR FOYER

FRENCH, CONTEMPORARY

WHILE THIS MODEL makes no pretense to set a standard for French decorative treatment during the 1920's or 30's, it does draw attention to some of the chief characteristics and virtues of its more conservative phases.

First is the striving for a simple and restful background stripped of nonessential ornament and pleasing on account of its interesting combination of textures. This is in harmony with the French classic tradition and has points of kinship with the basic feeling of much of the best work of about 1800. Upon this, we have the eclectic interests of our times with their far-reaching appreciation of the artistic contributions of cultures widely separated in both space and time. Modern French art has profited much from the lessons of the Orient.

In addition to this, the multiplication of techniques supplied by developments in science and industry have made possible textures and forms out of reach of the craftsman of other days. Some of these are here indicated in the wide veneering of the walls, and their obvious freedom from the limitations of masonry construction. The command of these new resources and facilities is, however, still to be learned.

As to the furniture, it is interesting to note that the Orient is responsible for such distinction as exists. The modern tendency to sparseness of furnishings is clearly evident.

The main decorative features as such are the needlework murals exquisitely representing the severe patterning of the school of Paris. Other accents are given in accord with the mode by independent sculptures and objects of art.

28. BOUDOIR—SITTING ROOM

GERMAN, EARLY NINETEENTH CENTURY, "BIEDERMEIER"

It was in rooms not unlike this that much of the finest music of the last century was heard for the first time.

The period following the Napoleonic wars was one of continued conflict in the realm of ideas. In the arts, the forms of classicism lingered, though their power was shaken by those romantic dreams and ideals that were also children of the French Revolution.

In the homes of the average citizen of the 1820's, 30's, and 40's, there was little opportunity for that ostentation which deprived those of the rich of the last traces of eighteenth-century charm.

In Germany, still a group of independent states, the man-on-the-street—his foibles and perplexities—was gently caricatured in the imaginary person of Papa Biedermeier. The everyday surroundings and possessions of this character, inheriting the name, were thus baptized in ridicule, though a century later received into honor.

Lately the name has been stretched to cover almost all middle-class European decorative arts of the romantic period. Under it is necessarily included much that is of no artistic value; but, in its positive aspects, it has furnished much fertile inspiration for contemporary work. Its simplicity, forced by economy, has produced, in many instances, designs of distinct personality with great charm of line. Through its mixed ancestry, it humanized the brittle quality of the late eighteenth-century survivals and reduced the pompousness of the Empire style into friendly and often gay forms that are at home in almost any company.

As to color, great latitude was allowed. Greens, blues, and browns predominated in harmony with the blond woods and tones prevailing in the furniture.

In terms of decoration, it typified the thrifty and sentimental qualities of the average man of the time with his quaint formalities surviving from the days "before the war." In this re-creation of the 1830's, Mrs. Thorne has combined the rather stiff arrangement usual at the time with a gracious quality of her own. The combination is irresistible.

Who today will not be envious of the beautiful tile stove!

29. "OUR LADY QUEEN OF ANGELS"

(Scale: ¾ inch equals 1 foot)

THIS MODEL, at a slightly smaller scale than the rest of the series, makes an appropriate termination to it.

The cultures represented by the rooms already discussed were, at base, dependent upon the stability of the Church, even after the dissensions of the Protestant movement. The Church was indeed the mother of the arts during at least three quarters of western European history.

This sanctuary is designed strictly in accord with the requirements of the Roman ritual as practiced today, which has changed comparatively little from that of the thirteenth and fourteenth centuries when the architectural and decorative forms used here were developed.

The model shows the last bay of the nave with quadripartite ribbed vaults, large clerestory windows above a low triforium, and a relatively low aisle arcade. It illustrates a phase of the English Gothic between that of the thirteenth century and the perpendicular style of the fourteenth.

The sanctuary beyond has a paneled wagon vault in wood and a blank wall instead of the customary east window above its reredos. In front of this is an elaborately carved reredos framing a painted altarpiece. Raised on three steps above the sanctuary floor is a free-standing altar.

On the right or Epistle side is a credence for the instruments of the sacrament, the official chair or sedile and the piscina. The doorway leads to the priest's chamber or sacristy. Above this, the pipes of the great organ are visible. On the left or Gospel side, a door leads to the vestry or working sacristy. A niche shelters the organ console with the ambry or cupboard for the holy oils in the wall beyond.

Below the chancel or triumphal arch hangs the rood cross. In early days, this was customarily flanked by images of the Virgin and St. John and below a screen of wood or stone protected the sanctuary from the vulgar gaze.

In the first bay of the nave arcade is a wrought iron grille in the fifteenth-century style which protects a side chapel dedicated to the Sacred Heart. On the opposite side is a doorway over which is carved one of the fourteen Stations of the Cross.

Note the absence of chairs or pews which are modern comforts. The only furniture in the nave are praying stands or *prie-dieu*.

30. CHINESE INTERIOR

As CHINESE HOUSES combine the residence and a place for worship, their plan and construction differ from those of the western world. This model is an example of a typical Chinese structure, representing, with only minor modifications, a plan which originated more than two thousand years ago.

It is divided into three parts: *Shang T'ang*, *Chung T'ang*, and *Hsia T'ang*—upper hall, central hall and lower hall, symbolic of Heaven, Earth and Humanity.

The *Shang T'ang*, or upper hall, is the most sacred part of the house. An ancestral portrait is hung in the center part of the wall, although occasionally an elaborate commemorative tablet is set into the wall. Here decorative urns and candlesticks are displayed in front of the portrait. Ancestral worship, New Year's celebrations, wedding and funeral rites are conducted in this hall.

The *Chung T'ang*, or central hall, is more narrow than the other halls. Here family treasures are stored in chests at either side. A few fine porcelains and paintings are displayed in this area.

The *Hsia T'ang*, or lower hall, is more properly the living area. It again is divided into three portions, one room on either side and an open court in the center, the latter providing light and air for the apartment. Favorite flowers and plants are also placed here for the enjoyment of the master and mistress who occupy the suite.

The woodwork and furniture are made of elaborately carved teakwood. It may be noted that the furniture is symmetrically arranged in formal groupings. The floor, finished to resemble brickwork, is covered with a handmade Chinese carpet.

31. JAPANESE INTERIOR

THIS MODEL IS a replica of a *zashiki*, or main room of a Japanese home, with an adjoining room customarily used by the mistress of the house.

The *tokonoma*, a niche where a painting is hung, and the companion bay called *tana*, a recess with artistically arranged wall-cupboards and shelves used to display a few objects of art, are essential in the planning of a *zashiki*. The floor is always covered with *tatami*, straw mats about three feet wide and six feet long, bound with borders of cotton cloth, usually black.

Simplicity and subdued color characterize this principal room of a Japanese dwelling. The room is opened to the garden and divided from the adjoining room by *shoji*, window-doors, and *fusuma*, interior partition-doors. These are made of light wood frames covered with paper, each measuring six feet in height and three feet in width.

The room is conspicuously bare of furniture, with the exception of a writing desk and low tables. Other accessories are brought in as the occasion demands. All of the objects used in this model room are replicas of larger pieces. The writing table is of fine black and gold lacquer, and the mirror and stand, made by the artist Yoshio, are of alloyed metal.